ASTROLOGY GEMS

TAURUS

April 20 – May 20

Monte Farber & Amy Zerner

Sterling Publishing Co., Inc.
New York

Text © 2006 by Monte Farber
Art © 2006 by Amy Zerner

10 9 8 7 6 5 4 3 2 1

Published by Sterling Publishing Co., Inc.
387 Park Avenue South, New York, NY 10016

Distributed in Canada by Sterling Publishing
c/o Canadian Manda Group, 165 Dufferin Street
Toronto, Ontario, Canada M6K 3H6

Distributed in the United Kingdom by GMC
Distribution Services
Castle Place, 166 High Street, Lewes, East Sussex,
England BN7 1XU

Distributed in Australia by Capricorn Link (Australia)
Pty. Ltd.
P.O. Box 704, Windsor, NSW 2756, Australia

Printed in China

Sterling ISBN-13: 978-1-4027-4185-2
        ISBN-10: 1-4027-4185-5

For information about custom editions, special sales,
premium and corporate purchases, please contact
Sterling Special Sales Department at 800-805-5489 or
specialsales@sterlingpub.com.

What's Your Sign?

When someone asks you "What's your sign?" you know what that person really means is "What's your astrological sign?" Professional astrologers more often use the phrase "Sun sign," a term reflecting the concept that a person's sign is determined by which of the twelve signs of the zodiac the Sun appeared to be passing through at the moment she was born. The zodiac is the narrow band of sky circling the Earth's equator through which the Sun, the Moon, and the planets appear to move when viewed by us here on Earth.

Astrology's Gift

Astrology, which has been around for thousands of years, is the study of how planetary positions relate to earthly events and people. Its long and rich history has resulted in a wealth of philosophical and psychological wisdom, the basic concepts of which we are going to share with you in the pages of this book. As the Greek philosopher Heracleitus (c. 540–c. 480 BCE) said, "Character is destiny." Who you are—complete with all of your goals, tendencies, habits, virtues, and vices—will

determine how you act and react, thereby creating your life's destiny. Like astrology itself, our Astrology Gems series is designed to help you to better know yourself and those you care about. You will then be better able to use your free will to shape your life to your liking.

Does Astrology Work?

Many people rightly question how astrology can divide humanity into twelve Sun signs and make predictions that can be correct for everyone of the same sign. The simple answer is that it cannot do that—that's newspaper astrology, entertaining but not the real thing. Rather, astrology can help you understand your strengths and weaknesses so that you can better accept yourself as you are and use your strengths to compensate for your weaknesses. Real astrology is designed to help you to become yourself fully.

Remember, virtually all the music in the history of Western music has been composed using variations of the same twelve notes. Similarly, the twelve Sun signs of astrology are basic themes rich with meaning that each of us expresses differently to create and respond to the unique opportunities and challenges of our life.

⟡ TAURUS ⟡

April 20–May 20

Planet
Venus

Element
Earth

Quality
Fixed

Day
Friday

Season
spring

Colors
spring green, blue, pink

Plants
daisy, magnolia, honeysuckle

Perfume
rose

Gemstones
moss agate, emerald, malachite,
rose quartz

Metal
copper

Personal qualities
Loyal, pragmatic, good-humored,
reliable, and musical

We call the following words "keywords" because they can help you unlock the core meaning of the astrological sign of Taurus. Each keyword represents issues and ideas that are of supreme importance and prominence in the lives of people born with Taurus as their Sun sign. You will usually find that every Taurus embodies at least one of these keywords in the way he makes a living:

slow and steady · values

money · nature · prosperity

caution · control · security

tenacity · texture · beauty

habits · supplies · kindness

calmness · romance · sensuality

sentimentality · harmony · food

organization · conservatism

hospitality · construction

working with minerals

Taurus' Symbolic Meaning

People born under this sign share many traits with their symbol, the Bull. Though usually patient and gentle, when pushed too far, Taureans can start to act like a bull tormented by a toreador's cape. Angry or not, they are so set on their goal that they can see little or nothing else. In fact, they sometimes think they must be equally set on the way in which they will accomplish their mission. Method is everything with Taurus. This can lead to stubbornness and an inability, or at least an unwillingness, to change.

Taureans seem to be able to cope with just about anything. In fact, they will exert the energy necessary to put up with a situation that those born under most other signs would just walk away from. But Taureans don't even like to walk around a situation, let alone walk away from it. Meeting challenges that require patience and endurance is how they prove their abilities to themselves and others.

Taurus is one of the four Fixed signs of the zodiac (the other three being Scorpio, Aquarius, and Leo). Fixed signs are stubborn, stable, and resolute. And they have an understanding of the material world.

Taurus is also one of the three Earth signs (the other two being Virgo and Capricorn). The Earth signs are concerned with the physical world—what they can see, feel, hear, and touch. Earth is a symbol of the environment in which growth takes place. The Earth signs embody the concepts of nurture, security, and protection. They embrace moderation and conservatism.

Taureans get the earthly comforts they need by exerting their immense power in a sustained and methodical manner, no matter who or what tries to make them deviate from their routine. They function best when they are able to concentrate and stick to a plan, especially when they know their reward will be pleasure and luxury. Spontaneity can be a stretch, even a challenge for them. While they may not be the first to jump at a new idea, once they get started they will embrace it and follow it through to the finish. They are dependable and extremely loyal—to ideas, traditions, and the people in their life.

Recognizing a Taurus

People who exhibit the physical characteristics distinctive of the sign of Taurus have kind eyes, round faces, and good complexions. They have sturdy, muscular, and compact bodies, and sometimes have wide feet and short hands. They like to wear accessories around their necks, as well as comfortable clothing made of sensual fabrics and earthy colors. They tend to put on weight if they don't exercise regularly, and move slowly, with determination.

Taurus' Typical Behavior and Personality Traits

- ❀ determined to succeed
- ❀ demonstrates shyness with new people
- ❀ copes well with difficult situations
- ❀ likes to sing
- ❀ is a deeply loyal friend
- ❀ possesses common sense
- ❀ likes good food and fine restaurants

- has a taste for luxury and beauty
- behaves in a pragmatic and stubborn manner
- works hard to build security
- assesses situations in financial terms
- is quiet and unpretentious
- can be wary and suspicious of others
- uses charm to get what he wants

What Makes a Taurus Tick?

Taureans value a middle-of-the-road approach to life. Not likely to get caught up in the latest trend, they believe in being themselves. Taureans need to understand that being true to their values does not mean they should be afraid to change their ideas or habits once in a while. They are not quick to engage in a confrontation, but swallowing too much anger can make them sick, literally and figuratively, or cause them to explode into a rage like a bull.

The Taurus Personality Expressed Positively

Taureans who are content with life radiate a glow of health and happiness. They are at their best when occupied with useful tasks that make their life and the lives of those around them more beautiful, harmonious, and fulfilling. Their ability to put events, both good and bad, into perspective allows them to see things practically, not emotionally.

On a Positive Note

Taureans displaying the positive characteristics associated with their sign also tend to be:

* patient and gentle

* attentive to aesthetics

* musically and artistically creative

* appreciative of the talents of others

* practical with resources

* good with plants and food

* demonstrative

* grounded and centered

* dependable with timing

The Taurus Personality Expressed Negatively

A Taurus who is either afraid of or uncomfortable with change displays one of the negative characteristics of the sign. Taureans may cling to traditional ideas more out of habit than principle. Even though this attitude may serve them well most of the time, it can also have a limiting effect on their progress and success.

Negative Traits

Taureans displaying the negative character-istics associated with their sign also tend to be:

❋ overly focused on material things

❋ too slow

❋ likely to stay in bad relationships too long

❋ possibly sloppy

❋ overly conservative

❋ embarrassed by free spirits

❋ skeptical

❋ self-indulgent

Ask a Taurus If...

Ask a Taurus if you want advice on how to increase your power and prestige. Taurus is never shy about giving tips and pointers, and will do it in such a nice way, you won't even realize you are being criticized. Thinking and planning in weeks instead of days, years instead of months, Taurus takes the long-term view of matters—and will expect you to do the same. The phrase "haste makes waste" expresses Taurus' viewpoint in a nutshell.

Taurus As Friends

Taureans make for gentle, charming, loving, and totally trustworthy friends. Because most Taurean individuals are unwilling to rely on others, they are usually very dependable themselves. A good Taurus will demonstrate a strong sense of loyalty to her friends. When it comes to friendship, Taurus looks for someone who is steady and devoted, and not given to panic or changes of plans. Those born under the sign of the Bull enjoy warm friendships with people who have good taste and with whom they can enjoy a good meal and converse about matters involving art, beauty, investments, and gardening. Highly affectionate toward their friends, Taureans enjoy calm, caring people who have the same qualities they do. The center of their universe is security, both physical and emotional, and through the gift of friendship they provide this treasure to others.

Looking for Love

Taureans enjoy simplicity. A Taurus will know he is in love when he just wants to be with a certain individual and watch that person live life naturally. Disliking signs of weakness, physical or emotional, a typical Taurus prizes a partner who has as strong a personality as he does. Taurus likes to share and savor power and resources. People who are rude, possess tacky taste, or have an unpleasant voice are unlikely to attract a Taurus.

Although Taureans are not usually picky, they do have certain standards. They don't like glib or shallow people, and it takes a great deal more than good looks and facile charm to turn their head. They enjoy compliments like anyone else, but they are much too level-headed to be taken in by them alone. Taureans are attracted to someone who is natural, plain-spoken, and sincere—someone who is not afraid to be herself.

Finding That Special Someone

To a Taurus, love is a natural, sensual, lusty experience that can be expected to last forever. A Taurus is attracted by physical beauty as well as by the successes and achievements of her partner. Romantic at heart, a Taurus is turned on by beautiful smells, flowers, colors, and music. Staying true to what she believes will improve a relationship greatly. When Taureans finally find their true love, they will achieve fulfillment.

First Dates

A good first date would be a concert or a football game, since Taurus loves music and enjoys any social, cultural, or sporting event. As far as choosing a restaurant is concerned, it is best if the Taurus picks the place or is consulted ahead of time, since those born under this sign are often excellent cooks and can be finicky about food. As Taureans can be reluctant conversationalists until they get to know a person better, they often won't share much personal information on a first date.

Taurus in Love

In love, Taurus has a slow, patient approach. It is important to Taurus that anyone he loves shares his personal tastes and desires. Taureans delight in deluxe comfort. So, for instance, although they love nature, they do not like to camp out. If a partner doesn't possess a similar love of comfort, there will eventually be a parting of the ways. When in love, Taureans are kind and gentle. They are natural and earthy in bed, and have a healthy self-image when it comes to their own body.

Undying Love

A Taurus can feel hurt and let down when she realizes that her partner is a human being with many faults. But a Taurus can also feel that she has to give the appearance of being blindly devoted to her partner, or to maintain some other kind of false personality, if the relationship is not going well. What Taurus really needs is a situation where each person loves the other for his or her true self; Taureans don't do well in relationships where each individual is trying to change the other.

Taurus needs to seek a relationship that is a union of two independent people who are secure in as many ways as possible. Being with someone not because of who they are but because of what that person can offer will not lead to happiness.

Expectations in Love

Taureans believe in setting high standards, especially at the beginning of a relationship. Their fundamental concern is that their love be grounded in reality, and that they not become involved in some sort of superficial infatuation that won't last. Because they have generally realistic expectations about romance, Taureans are seldom disappointed in love. They are not likely to be drawn into a relationship that is based solely on lust and good times, nor do they expect any love affair that begins on that note to grow into something deeper and more significant.

For Taurus, loyalty is paramount in a relationship. They expect their ideas, desires, and dreams to be applauded and supported. They also like to receive sincere compliments on their appearance and accomplishments.

What Taurus Looks For

Taureans require harmony with a partner. While they don't expect to be agreed with at every turn, they want the sort of relationship where any sort of dispute is handled with respect and good humor. Taureans can have their head turned by good looks, but only if the person they are attracted to has an equally beautiful spirit. They appreciate intelligence but are not likely to be attracted to someone who shows off their knowledge.

If Taurus Only Knew…

If Taureans only knew that their home-spun wisdom was held in such high esteem by the individuals who deal with them, they would stop secretly wondering if others find them interesting. While Taureans are comfortable with their communication skills, they may not feel that they are as witty and wise as other people. They need to realize that it is the strength and sincerity of their speech that makes the emotions they convey so believable and endearing.

Marriage

Taureans are stable, commonsense people who value home and family. While they make devoted partners, they can also be deeply possessive. Taureans like to be appreciated, and they believe in expensive gifts. No partner can force a Taurus into making a decision without allowing time for thought and consideration. That said, Taureans are highly capable and have an instinctive understanding of what to do in important situations. Partial to creature comforts, they like their home to be elegant and beautiful. Not surprisingly, Bulls are often bullheaded about their opinions, which can sometimes lead to incidences of emotional bullying, although these are rare. Sexually, they are intense, yet gentle.

Taurus' Opposite Sign

Scorpio is the opposite sign of Taurus. Because both signs are stubborn, relations between the two can be difficult. However, Scorpio can show a Taurus how to gain insight into the needs and motives of other people, and ultimately into the Taurus' own life. While Scorpio's intensity and drive mirror Taurus' determination, the Bull can learn a great deal about the spiritual terrain of love and commitment from Scorpio. Like Taurus, Scorpio is slow to forgive.

Pairing Up

In general, if people display the characteristics typical of their sign, intimate relationships between a Taurus and another individual can be described as follows:

Taurus with Taurus
Harmonious, but can sometimes be lacking in excitement

Taurus with Gemini
Harmonious, despite considerable differences in personality

Taurus with Cancer
Harmonious because Taurus understands Cancer's sensitivity

Taurus with Leo
Difficult, with arguments about money being a constant factor

Taurus with Virgo
Harmonious in the extreme—a very tender love story

Taurus with Libra
Turbulent yet affectionate and passionate

Taurus with Scorpio
Difficult in the extreme, with periods of obsessive passion

Taurus with Sagittarius
Turbulent if Taurus attempts to make Sagittarius conform

Taurus with Capricorn
Harmonious, due to comparable
values and goals

Taurus with Aquarius
Difficult, but a sense of humor is a
big help

Taurus with Pisces
Harmonious, with both partners
supporting each other's dreams

Taurus with Aries
Harmonious, but requiring a respect
for boundaries

If Things Don't Work Out

When Taureans are comfortable in a romantic relationship, it can be difficult for them to deal with the idea of changing the status quo, even when the relationship is not working. As a result, they tend to keep their unhappiness and disappointment bottled up inside, hoping that things will get better. However, once they come to understand that the only way to reclaim their own power is by leaving the relationship gone bad, they will do so without wringing their hands over the consequences.

Taurus at Work

Never flashy or dramatic, Taureans believe in getting the job accomplished through hard work and dedicated persistence. It is not necessary or even important for them to receive accolades for their performance in the workplace. Just knowing that they are doing a good job and earning their paycheck is enough for them.

The congenial personality that Taureans tend to possess is a big plus in the workplace. Reliable, unflappable, and graced with a professional attitude, they make excellent personal assistants. No matter how many tasks they are expected to finish in a given day, they never appear to be overwhelmed. Because of their discretion, they can be counted on to keep the confidences entrusted to them by an employer. They are not likely to gossip or get involved in cliques.

Even though they are independent minded and set in their ways, Taureans make excellent team players because they never put anything above getting the job done. While it can be hard at first to convince them to handle a task in a way that is foreign to them, they will gladly fall into line once they have been made to understand that this method will improve chances for accomplishing a goal in a way that benefits everyone concerned.

Typical Occupations

Taureans do well in banking and finance, transportation, construction, conservation, landscaping, farming, engineering, and mathematics. The sign is also associated with floristry, food, general medical practice, executive secretarial positions, stable occupations in established institutions, and any type of job that involves land, investments, minerals, or other hard goods. They have a natural affinity for working with their hands. Careers that help to make someone's environment more beautiful and harmonious are particularly relevant to them.

Thoroughness and single-mindedness that can become dogmatic are well-known traits of the persistent Taurus personality. No detail will ever be over-looked. Interior design, architecture, and the fine arts—especially sculpture, fashion, music, and singing—are also good fields for Bulls. Often graced with pleasant speaking voices, they do well in sales or any work that requires a lot of oratory.

Details, Details

Taureans can appreciate the saying "God is in the details" more than those born under almost any other sign. While they can appear to work in a slow, even plodding way, Taureans believe that it is better to take a little longer to accomplish a chore than to speed through a task and make mistakes.

Some signs may find details boring, but Taurus never does. In fact, it is in details that he is able to see the overall significance of a project. Taurus possesses a natural ability to work with figures. The

Bull is much better at acting as a facilitator of someone else's ideas than at being the "idea person" behind a project. They will not feel insulted or demoted in any way if they are assigned work that is largely detail oriented, rather than creative in nature.

Taureans will seldom miss a day of work. This is a result of not only loyalty and good habits, but also the understanding that the best work is accomplished over the long haul. Taurus' self-esteem improves when he feels good about the job he does.

Behavior and Abilities at Work

In the workplace, a typical Taurus:

❀ values tradition

❀ hates to be interrupted

❀ demonstrates a steady and reliable work ethic

❀ requires a routine and a plan

❀ stays on schedule

❀ does not give up

❀ needs clear goals

Taurus As Employer

A typical Taurus boss:

❀ is a good judge of character

❀ works to increase income for the company

❀ looks for loyalty and honesty

❀ does not make hasty decisions

❀ expects to be respected

❀ won't budge if pushed

❀ cannot be manipulated

Taurus As Employee

A typical Taurus employee:

- doesn't like freelance jobs

- behaves honestly

- deals with matters in a down-to-earth and sensible way

- demonstrates punctuality

- will rarely be pushed to anger

- excels when it comes to dealing with numbers

Taurus As Coworker

Taureans believe in compartmentalizing their lives, so they are just as unlikely to bring work problems home as they are to discuss personal matters at work. Although friendly and pleasant, they seldom develop deep friendships with coworkers.

Money

Extremely risk averse, Taurus is not the type for gambling of any sort. Yet, motivated by a desire to obtain and accumulate material possessions, Taureans can be compulsive in their intensity to secure an ample supply of the things they consider important to their comfort and happiness. Worrying about money can be highly stressful for them, so they should not attempt to stretch their resources to the limit. Taureans should put money in safe and secure investments such as a savings account or IRA, rather than attempt to be a financial wizard. Existing financial resources should be properly allocated, used, and developed. Some Taureans will envy the resources of their richer friends or family members, but most appreciate the wisdom of being satisfied with the good things they already possess.

At Home

For Taureans, home is a place to feel absolutely secure. Beauty is an important component of their surroundings, but comfort is an even more valuable asset. Cooking, cleaning, and working in the garden are more appealing to most Taureans than engaging in social activities.

Behavior and Abilities at Home

Taurus typically:

❀ enjoys do-it-yourself repairs

❀ is adept at planning nutritious menus

❀ runs a well-organized home

❀ likes to be in charge of decorating projects

❀ believes that harmony is expressed through color

Leisure Interests

Beautifying the home, office, and backyard, or going to a concert, play, art exhibit, or any other cultural event are activities that Taureans are likely to enjoy, as long as they are able to relax, take their time, and savor the beauty and creativity of the experience. At home, Bulls like to settle back on a nice cozy couch, listening to their favorite music or watching a romantic DVD.

The typical Taurus enjoys the following pastimes:

- ❀ expanding a music collection
- ❀ craft and art projects
- ❀ home improvement projects
- ❀ working with plants and flowers
- ❀ counting money
- ❀ taking naps

Taurean Likes

* jewelry

* sculpture

* gardens

* sensual colors and shapes

* a regular routine

* a wonderful meal

* attractive surroundings

* expensive birthday presents

* vacations

* chocolate

Taurean Dislikes

- ❀ abrupt changes of plans

- ❀ lending or borrowing

- ❀ rushing to get ready

- ❀ clashing colors

- ❀ eating on the run

- ❀ dissonant music

- ❀ being late

The Secret Side of Taurus

Taureans love the best things in life, and long to be rich, retired, and surrounded by beauty. But they secretly fear that they won't have enough material resources to make their dreams come true. Those born under this sign like to appear cool, calm, and collected. But when they do eventually express anger, it can be devastating to those around them and so disturbing to themselves that it takes a while for them to recover both their composure and their self-esteem.

Venus ♀

Venus—known in astrology as the planet of love, affection, values, and sensuality—rules the sign of Taurus. Sociable Venus also rules over parties and pleasurable meetings. She accomplishes her goals by attracting only what she wants and rejecting the rest, thus making taste and values two of her special talents. The love and beauty of Venus have the power to both unite and heal us. Venus also rules our senses of touch, taste, and smell.

Like Venus, Taurus can be highly affectionate and fond of the good life, as long as it is a peaceful, secure existence. Taureans rarely deviate from their personal code of what is right, even in the search for pleasure. Those whose birth charts have a strong Taurus influence tend to possess a firm set of personal values.

Bringing Up a Young Taurus

Young Taurean children respond to practical direction and common sense. They don't like to be pushed or forced, but instead tend to listen and respond to calm and gentle direction, especially if it is delivered with patience and a soft tone of voice. Generally well behaved and sweet tempered, Taurean children can also be highly stubborn and will dig in their heels when confronted with new challenges, such as sharing with other children. Take your time with Taurean youngsters, as the slow-and-steady approach works best. In dealings with them, stressing routine and sticking with established goals are advantageous.

Physical affection is essential to the healthy growth of any Taurean child. Young Taurus also needs a harmonious environment in which to flourish. Colors, sounds, and smells will affect these children quite deeply. Surrounding them with shades of spring green, light blue, pink, and rose, as well as soft music, provides reassurance and comfort.

It is good to teach Taurean children about the importance of ethics and commitment. Teaching by example is crucial and will result in their learning important lessons that they can take into their teen years and adulthood.

Taurus As a Parent

The typical Taurus parent:

- ❀ is judicious in dispensing discipline

- ❀ encourages music lessons

- ❀ believes in taking children to cultural events

- ❀ teaches the importance of good grooming

- ❀ enjoys singing to her child

- ❀ encourages his child to have friends

- ❀ creates an atmosphere of harmony at home

The Taurus Child

The typical Taurus child:

✺ responds to comfort and affection

✺ is generally good-natured

✺ may excel in singing or other forms of music

✺ possesses more strength than one would suspect

✺ is usually cuddly, calm, and affectionate

✺ can be obstinate

- ✹ may dislike scratchy or woolen clothes

- ✹ may be prone to sore throats

- ✹ usually works slowly but steadily at school

- ✹ may be selfish with toys or other possessions

- ✹ should be encouraged to play sports

- ✹ is likely to have many friends

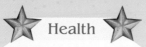

Health

Taureans usually enjoy good health throughout their lives, but when they do experience issues, the problems tend to occur in the sinus area, throat, and lungs. These parts of the body can be subject to repeated infections. Neck and voice problems are also common complaints, as the body part that Taurus rules is the neck.

Taureans tend to like sweet desserts, which, eaten frequently or in abundance, can eventually lead to weight issues. Fatty, high-calorie cuisine should be avoided. Taureans should also stay away from foods that are high in sodium or caffeine, as these can have a troublesome effect on their systems. To maintain their health, Bulls should exercise regularly, and, in particular, should take long walks. Taurus loves the outdoors, so meditative time spent in gardens and fresh air would be a healthy habit to develop.

⭐ FAMOUS TAUREANS ⭐

David Beckham

Candice Bergen

Pierce Brosnan

James Brown

Carol Burnett

Catherine the Great

Cher

Kelly Clarkson

Penelope Cruz

Salvador Dalí

Tony Danza

Queen Elizabeth II

Sigmund Freud

Audrey Hepburn

Jay Leno

Shirley MacLaine

Tim McGraw

Willie Nelson

Jack Nicholson

Al Pacino

Michelle Pfeiffer

William Shakespeare

Barbra Streisand

Uma Thurman

Orson Welles

About the Authors

Internationally known self-help author Monte Farber's inspiring guidance and empathic insights impact everyone he encounters. Amy Zerner's exquisite one-of-a-kind spiritual couture creations and collaged fabric paintings exude her profound intuition and deep connection with archetypal stories and healing energies. Together, they have built The Enchanted World of Amy Zerner and Monte Farber: books, card decks, and

oracles that have helped millions discover their own spiritual paths.

Their best-selling titles include The Chakra Meditation Kit, The Enchanted Tarot, The Instant Tarot Reader, The Psychic Circle, Karma Cards, The Truth Fairy, The Healing Deck, True Love Tarot, Animal Powers Meditation Kit, The Breathe Easy Deck, The Pathfinder Psychic Talking Board, and Gifts of the Goddess Affirmation Cards.

For further information, please visit: www.TheEnchantedWorld.com